All Kinds of Friends

My Friend Has Autism

by Kaitlyn Duling

Bullfrog Books

Ideas for Parents and Teachers

Bullfrog Books let children practice reading informational text at the earliest reading levels. Repetition, familiar words, and photo labels support early readers.

Before Reading

- Discuss the cover photo. What does it tell them?

- Look at the picture glossary together. Read and discuss the words.

Read the Book

- "Walk" through the book and look at the photos. Let the child ask questions. Point out the photo labels.

- Read the book to the child, or have him or her read independently.

After Reading

- Prompt the child to think more. Ask: Do you know someone with autism? How can you be a good friend to him or her?

Bullfrog Books are published by Jump!
5357 Penn Avenue South
Minneapolis, MN 55419
www.jumplibrary.com

Library of Congress Cataloging-in-Publication Data

Names: Duling, Kaitlyn, author.
Title: My friend has autism / by Kaitlyn Duling.
Description: Minneapolis, MN: Jump!, Inc., 2020.
Series: All kinds of friends
Includes bibliographical references and index.
Audience: Age 5–8. | Audience: K to Grade 3.
Identifiers: LCCN 2018052796 (print)
LCCN 2018055774 (ebook)
ISBN 9781641287319 (ebook)
ISBN 9781641287296 (hardcover : alk. paper)
ISBN 9781641287302 (pbk.)
Subjects: LCSH: Autism—Juvenile literature.
Autistic children—Juvenile literature.
Friendship—Juvenile literature.
Classification: LCC RC553.A88 (ebook)
LCC RC553.A88 D847 2019 (print) | DDC 618.92/85882—dc23
LC record available at https://lccn.loc.gov/2018052796

Editor: Susanne Bushman
Designer: Molly Ballanger

Special thanks to the staff of the Minneapolis Southwest High School Special Ed Program

Photo Credits: Tad Saddoris, cover, 3, 8, 9, 23br; yellowsarah/iStock, 1; ChiccoDodiFC/Shutterstock, 4, 5; AMELIE-BENOIST/BSIP/SuperStock, 6–7, 23tr; pick-uppath/iStock, 10; Monkey Business Images/Shutterstock, 10–11; Photographee.eu/Shutterstock, 12–13, 23tl; Olesia Bilkei/Shutterstock, 14; Ranta Images/Shutterstock, 15; wavebreakmedia/Shutterstock, 16–17, 23bl; Veja/Shutterstock, 18–19 (table); Sorapop Udomsri/Shutterstock, 18–19 (tablet); fstop123/iStock, 20–21; dantess/Shutterstock, 22tl; Jolanta Beinarovica/Shutterstock, 22tr; IrynaL/Shutterstock, 22bl; Molly Ballanger, 22br; Special Olympics, 24.

Printed in the United States of America at Corporate Graphics in North Mankato, Minnesota

Table of Contents

This is Bree.

She has autism.

Some things are hard for her.

In many ways,
she is just like us.

We play. Fun!

People with autism
aren't all the same.

They all have
different abilities.

Just like us!

Lily flaps
her arms.

She is excited!

Max wears a vest.

Why?

It helps him feel good!

vest

9

Bright lights upset Lee.

We turn some off.

This helps my friend.

aide

Ron has an aide.

She is his helper.

She helps him learn.

Nice!

Mac can be quiet.
He doesn't look
at my eyes.

14

Noisy rooms bother him.

We talk quietly.

15

We work together.

We use TJ's tablet.

tablet

TJ taps the screen.

He uses it to talk to us.

It says, "Let's play!"

Cool!

We are all different.
We are all friends!

Helpful Tools

headphones
Headphones block out noises and help with focus.

sensory toys
Sensory toys appeal to the senses and help with concentration.

tablet
Tablets help people with autism communicate with friends and family.

weighted vest
Weighted vests give comfort and help with focus.

Picture Glossary

aide
An adult who helps out in the classroom or at home.

autism
A condition that can cause a range of communication and behavioral challenges.

tablet
A flat computer with a touchscreen that you can carry with you.

vest
A piece of clothing without sleeves that is sometimes weighted and is used to comfort people with autism.

Index

To Learn More

Finding more information is as easy as 1, 2, 3.

❶ Go to www.factsurfer.com

❷ Enter "myfriendhasautism" into the search box.

❸ Choose your book to see a list of websites.

FACT SURFER